Hatfield Peverel

in old picture postcards volume 1

by Joyce P. Fitch

European Library ZALTBOMMEL/THE NETHERLANDS

GB ISBN 90 288 6141 6

© 1995 European Library – Zaltbommel/The Netherlands

Fourth edition, 1999: reprint of the original edition of 1995.

Introduction

At the very heart of Essex lies Hatfield Peverel. The parish is roughly square in shape, with the greatest proportion of inhabitants living south of the old Roman Road from London to Colchester and east of the River Ter. Today it is bypassed by the A12.

Roman soldiers marched along the Street and their artefacts have been found in the village; together with the Saxons and Normans they were largely instrumental in the formation of the village that we know today. Links with the first Norman king, William the Conqueror, and his beautiful Saxon mistress, Ingelrica, conjure up a sense of romance that has never quite died. When William tired of Ingelrica, herself of noble birth, he married her off to Ranulph de Peverel, a favourite knight, who had distinguished himself at the Battle of Hastings in 1066. It is to Ingelrica's Saxon race that we owe the first known name of the village, *Hadfelda*, which is recorded in the Domesday Book of 1086 and means: *a clearing in the wild uncultivated ground*. It is to Ranulph that we owe the name, *Peverel*.

What a tiny community it must have been then. History tells us that Ingelrica, repenting of past misdoings, founded a College of Secular Canons in the village. After her death around 1100, her son, William Peverel, changed and enlarged this to a Benedictine priory of which only the parish church remains.

In 1566 Hatfield Peverel, a village of around 500 souls, found itself at the centre of a storm concerning three women, each accused of being a witch. They were tried at Chelmsford and one, Agnes Waterhouse, was found guilty and hanged. Thus the village holds the dubious honour of being home to one of the first Essex inhabitants to die on a charge of witchcraft.

Slowly, oh so slowly, the population grew. By 1801, around 250 years later, it had reached a figure of 1,008 taking another century to climb to 1,204. By the year 1951 that figure had doubled to 2,285, since when it has rocketed to stand today at around 4,500.

It is with the period 1880-1930, that this book is concerned. Until the onset of the First World War the pace of life was slow and most men worked on the land in a village which was largely self-sufficient. Only rarely did people need to visit the nearby towns of Chelmsford, Witham and Maldon as a matter of necessity. No villager born at the beginning of the century believed that life would ever be any different from the one he knew. In a trade directory of 1891 are listed many age-old trades and professions no longer to be found in the village. Among them are: a saddler, two wheelwrights, two drapers, two millers, a veterinary surgeon, a ratcatcher, three boot and shoemakers, two blacksmiths, a horse slaughterer, a brickmaker and a brewer. By 1937 only half of these are still listed and today there are none. Photographs of some of these people or their place of work appear in the pages that follow.

Because early photographic plates took longer to develop it was essential for the subject to remain motionless, resulting in figures which often appear very posed and stiff. To move would have been to blur the image. Fred Spalding of Chelmsford was an acknowledged master of his craft, as was his son, Fred Spalding junior, and we owe them both a big debt of gratitude, not only for the clarity of their pictures but for their eye for design. To add interest to skies, Spalding senior often drew in birds – watch out for them in one of his cards. Three early photographers from Witham surnamed Afford, Hall and Bull and, later, two local men, Cyril Wise and Clifford Dawson, all captured on film and published as postcards, many places in the village that have passed into oblivion. There is one other, unknown, photographer whose work the reader may identify by the digits '769' which prefix the number on each of his cards. Six cards are reproduced here of which only one (No. 46.) was posted. It bore a stamp franked in 1916, from which it has been possible to date, approximately, the other five. Even with one such postmark, accurate dating of other photographs is not always possible, for one of the cards Fred Spalding produced was still being posted ten years after it first appeared. Until a telephone exchange was installed at Hatfield Peverel in 1915 the postcard was a convenient and cheap form of communication. The messages on the backs make fascinating reading and range through several topics: birthday greetings, news of the harvest, a girl in service writing home, and a proposed visit for the following day giving train times. Almost all make mention of the state of the weather.

Although this is not a history book in the serious sense of the word, the postcards, nevertheless, record an important part of the social history of the period. Large families were common at the end of the 1800s and houses were often overcrowded. Many were in a sorry state, a hazard to health and unfit for human habitation at a time when sanitary arrangements were virtually non-existent. Local newspapers of the time carry reports of the dangers of sewage from roadside ditches seeping into wells, when there was, of course, no piped water supply. Elderly villagers' memories of these conditions are still vivid. It was not until the early 1920s, when Braintree Rural District Council began the building of houses on the Green that things began to improve. But sadly, as tenants moved out into brand new homes, the prohibitive cost of renovation meant that many of the centuries-old, and picturesque houses in the village were demolished. From a wealth of cards it has been difficult to decide which to include. A pleasant route to take seemed a gentle stroll along the Street from the top of Crix Hill, making a little diversion by way of Station Road, eventually to arrive at the Duke of Wellington public house. We continue at a leisurely pace along Maldon Road and Church Road before reaching the Green and Nounsley.

In some of the postcards there is much fascinating detail not easily discernible to the naked eye; by the use of strong magnification I have been able to provide additional, less obvious information which I hope will interest the reader. A modest magnifying glass will often reveal unexpected delights and its occasional use is a practice I would recommend.

In order to capture the spirit of the time I have chatted with thirty or more of the older inhabitants, who, as children, kicked a ball, bowled a hoop or whipped a spinning top along the empty roads. Almost all were born in Hatfield Peverel and have spent their lives here. To accompany the photographs I have endeavoured, from their recollections and the official documents I have examined over many years, to put together an account of the life they lived. Most of the photographs properly depict a peaceful and ordered scene of rural life, and in many instances that is exactly how it was. But there were also concentrated areas of great activity. Near the junction of the Maldon Road with the Street was such an area, for, within a few yards of each other, were a blacksmith, a wheelwright, a coachbuilder, and the baker-cum-postmaster. As you peruse the pictures, smell the acrid smoke of horses being shod with red-hot shoes and feel the heat from the two fires inside the forge. Smell the delicate scent of wood-shavings as a waggon takes on shape, and smell the warm aroma of bread, newly-baked, that wafts from the bakehouse next door. Hear the ring of hammer on anvil and the hammering home of nails. Listen to the tramp of heavy boots as never ending columns of soldiers march along the Street to war. In 1916 no fewer than 6,000 are reported stationed here in homes and barns, or

encamped in fields. Then take yourself off to the Green and stand outside the brewery. Breathe in the sweet smell of fermenting hops and listen to the clatter of barrels as they are rolled up from the cellar and on
to awaiting horse-drawn drays.

One theme was common to all tales of the earlier years of this century:
life was more simple then, even though it was hard, and people
seemed happier and content with their lot.

In the writing of this book I have received encouragement and support
from many people and I sincerely thank them all. Particularly I wish to
express gratitude to the following: the Staff of the Essex Record Office;
B.T. Archives and The National Motor Museum at Beaulieu. Mr. Stan Jar-
vis gave me wise advice and my husband, Mick, a tower of strength,
saw to it that I sometimes ate. Forty-five people trusted me with pre-
cious cards, photographs and newscuttings, while over thirty more
readily shared with me their invaluable recollections. To all of these,
and to Derek Gratze and Lynne and Mick Mickelsen, must go my warm
appreciation. Special thanks go to Mr. E. Springett, born in 1899, who,
during several visits, took me in memory, still crystal-clear, on a tour of
the village as it was when this century began. To Mr. Eric Morley, with
his photographic expertise, I owe a great deal. He cheerfully listened,
copied, advised and revised, while his wife, Heather, made us both
endless cups of coffee. Lastly, although every effort has been made to
cross-match memories and verify facts, it is inevitable that recollections
of events long ago may differ.

I do hope that your browse through this book of Hatfield Peverel past
will afford you much pleasure.

Hatfield Peverel, Joyce P. Fitch

1   Seated regally at the Chelmsford approach to the village, and set back from the old Roman Road, the fine Georgian mansion called Crix is reached from either end of a gracefully curving drive. Here, around 1905, Fred Spalding has captured its air of spaciousness. In 1930 Miss Teresa M. Hope, who lived at Crix, published her book *The Township of Hatfield Peverel*, in which she tells of Walter de Creyk, who held land here in the mid-1200s. The present house, built on the orders of Mr. Samuel Shaen, the then owner, dates from the late 1700s when it was fashionable to build with bricks of white or yellow. Disdaining fashion Crix was constructed using brick of a pleasing red. Associated with the house is the story of Shaen's Shaggy Dog, a big dog with glaring eyes that was said to haunt the area between the two drive-gates. The driver of a timber wain lashed out at him with his whip: driver, whip, horses, load and waggon were burnt to ashes.

CRIX

Fred Spalding
Photo
Chelmsford
copyright

2 In this postcard of 1916 we have reached the bottom of the hill where the river Ter flows sweetly alongside the road. Behind its border of wooden rustic fencing, trout swim in its waters and lilies float on its surface. In this scene of utter tranquillity the brilliant colours of the kingfisher flash for an instant and are gone. The driver of a twin-cylinder Humberette is out for a leisurely drive and trees cast dappled shadows. As we approach the village we draw near to the Mill House and then the Mill itself. The House had an interior chimney stack inscribed with the date, 1715, and the letters A.A. (Arabella Alleyn). The Mill was demolished in 1931 when Mr. Kenneth McCorquodale, the owner, considered it unsafe, but the Mill House survived another thirty years before being pulled down during preparatory work on the A12 bypass. The course of the river was then entirely diverted, its bed filled in and this beautiful view was lost forever.

HATFIELD PEVEREL. 18954

3   Hatfield Mill was an impressive structure, Five storeys high and with walls one and a half feet thick, it was built about 1790 of brick and deal and stood for around 140 years. On its imminent demolition in 1931 the *Essex Weekly News* carried an obituary. The Mill was used originally to grind corn but for a while it changed to silk weaving before once more reverting to corn. Working conditions in the silk mill must have been abysmal, for the *Colchester Gazette* (1825) reported that fifty girls absconded, one saying that she worked six days per week 6 a.m. to 7 p.m. with half hour breaks for breakfast and dinner. From her weekly wage of 3s. 6d. in the first year and 4s. in the second year she paid 1s. 0d. for lodging, 2s. 6d. for food and clothes and had little to eat but bread. She was sentenced to seven days hard labour.

4   The Spaldings must have been enchanted by the rural beauty of the Mill for it was photographed time and time again. Here, as we begin the ascent of Hatfield Hill, we turn to look back at the scene that caught their eye. Shaded by trees, the River Ter gently runs its course beneath the bridge of brick in the centre foreground, before turning into a torrent in the turbulence of the Mill race. The road beyond lies roughly at the spot where the old Roman Road and the sliproad to the A12 bypass today part company. The Mill and cottages adjoining stood directly on the road, and here, frozen forever on film, a driver anticipates a delivery of flour to be lowered into the empty waggon beside him. His horse patiently awaits both load and master. No motorised traffic detracts from the peaceful charm of this picture.

HATFIELD PEVEREL. 1792.

HATFIELD PEVEREL. 510.

5 Dated 1927, this card was posted three years after Ernie Williams came with his family to live in the further of these two brick and tile cottages. Mr. Williams was gardener at Hatfield Place and Mr. Clements, who moved in next door a few years later, was both groom and chauffeur. Beneath the fairy-tale style, six-sided roofs of this pair of cottages, at some time called Greystones, were rooms of the same shape. As we look back toward the river, they stood exactly opposite the lower of the two drive gates leading to the big house itself. In 1961, following road widening, the area at the bottom of the hill was prepared for a much-needed village bypass. The course of the river was diverted and the fate of these two delightful little cottages was sealed. Along with the Mill House and two other houses whose front doors opened directly on to the road, they were demolished, bringing a small, close-knit community abruptly to an end.

HATFIELD PEVEREL

6   Halfway up Hatfield Hill above the river Ter and on the right of the road, stands Hatfield Place. It replaced a farmhouse called Ponds, located nearer the river. Hidden by trees, this elegant house as photographed by Spalding around 1906, may today be seen to better advantage from the public footpath running beside the grounds. It was the first house in the village to have electricity, Mr. David Pease being instrumental in ingeniously harnessing river water to provide the power for Colonel Arkwright, then owner of both Mill and Hatfield Place. In 1924 a Grand Pageant of the history of the village was staged by the Women's Institute in a field at the back. Months of preparation were involved with men, women and children from all walks of life taking part. It had a cast of 150, was performed on two days and ended with a torchlight procession. Villagers still talk of it with pleasure today.

HATFIELD PLACE, ESSEX. 438.

Fred Spalding
Photo...
Chelmsford.
Copyright.

7   As the motor car grew in popularity the Crown Inn became a favourite spot to partake of refreshment. In this card postmarked May 1927, a proud owner poses beside his vehicle – probably a 10.5 h.p. Calcott, while the larger car in front is possibly a Sunbeam. A bicycle and a lorry provide more modest transport. The Crown served not only beer, it also served teas in the little garden on the extreme left, reached by some small brick steps. Now called the William Boosey, the pub stands on the right side of the old Roman road at the top of Hatfield Hill on the approach from Chelmsford. Originally it was a pair of cottages. In 1641 a William Boosey is mentioned in the Quarter Sessions as having enlarged the property and 'receiving of inmates' evidence of its being used as an inn. At that time it was known as 'The Drumme'. Kelly's Directory for 1899 lists Mrs. Mary Ann Baring as keeper of 'The Crown'.

LUNCHEONS.
FULLY LICENSED.

THE CROWN,
HATFIELD PEVEREL,
NR. CHELMSFORD.

TEAS.
GARAGE.

PROPRIETOR. JOHN. G. BOLINGBROKE.

8 The small, neat house with its ivy-clad walls, seen here in 1916, is known as Walnut Tree Cottage. The little shop adjoining, with blinds shading the window, is part of the same property. Over the years this shop has rung the changes many times in its diversity of trades. It has been a dame school, tea shop, a wool shop, an ironmonger's and a draper's. In 1920, Mr. Lynes ran the ironmonger's in one half of the shop while his wife busied herself with the drapery in the other. They later moved to Wisteria Cottage (see No. 27). At that time, Mr. Herbert Springett carried on an early omnibus company transporting passengers to and from Notley and Brain-tree from his premises just out of sight on the left. A cart horse emerges from Bury Lane while beyond is the Chapel steeple. On the opposite side of the road runs the garden wall of Hill House, its cellars once reputed to be a cache for smugglers' contraband.

9   Originally three cottages, this long, white-fronted house is now one dwelling with an address of 12-14 the Street. Earlier it formed part of the adjacent property, Walnut Tree Cottage, described in the preceding entry. Over three hundred years ago, in a court document of 1657, it was called 'The Starr' when a seaman, named Thomas Viner, *being att the signe of the Starr, an Alehouse in Hatfeild … did take one hatt, a close coate, a paire of breeches and a paire of Jersey stockings* from William Atkeeler, bricklayer, who had given him lodging. His punishment is not known. In 1886, Mrs. White, an occupant of almost two hundred and thirty years later, keeps a shopping book (found in the skirting board) which records: … *2 pints peas, 5d., blacking (for the stove) 1d., ¼ yd velvet, 9d., ¾ lb cheese 6d and ¼ lb tea, also costing 6d.* These assorted purchases would have been bought from shops nearby (see Nos. 12 and 16).

10 This fine old house and butcher's shop stood at the junction of Bury Lane (extreme left edge) with the Street. It was taken about midday with the sun shining on the joints of meat displayed in the window and at some time before 1908 when the present shop was built. The well-built gentleman was Mr. John Steele, butcher, who lived at Terling, and he stands beside his young assistant. Occasionally a drunken fight would break out at the local hostelry whereupon the landlord would send for John. Standing 6 feet 2 inches tall in his stockinged feet and weighing 18 ½ stones, he would grab the miscreants by the scruff of the neck, lift them up and bang their heads together before carting them off to Witham police station. The new premises were first occupied by Mr. R. Sorrell, (whose phone number in 1920 was Hatfield Peverel 9) then Mr. Stevens (both butchers), before becoming Jonathans Estate Agents. Today it stands empty.

11   To take this picture of 1905, the photographer must have stood in the centre of the now busy junction near Bury Lane where the A12 sliproad meets the Street. The fence on the left fronts John Steele's shop (see No. 10). Next door, with its advertisement for Quaker Oats on the side wall and a tin bath on the ground at the front to catch rainwater, is the general store of Walter J. Clarke. Today it is the Post Office. Beyond is the spire of the Methodist Chapel while on the right, the oriel windows of David Doe, shoemaker, project over the pavement – just as they do today. In the gap that follows there once stood a pair of houses, long since gone. Three lath and plaster houses, built in 1702 and pulled down about 1912, stand on the former site of the old Village Hall. This was erected in 1920 and in its turn demolished (see No. 15). One small boy, in no danger from traffic, stands posed for the photographer.

Hatfield-Peverel, Essex.   Afford, Stationer, Witham.

12　We will look more closely at the shop in the foreground, referred to in card No. 9. The name above the window is that of Mr. Walter Clarke, but it was his wife, Ada, who ran the business while her husband worked at his forge (see No. 16). Mrs. Clarke sold everything from calico to candles, and paraffin to clothes pegs; in the window are ready-to-wear garments with rolls of material stacked on the shelf above. Sides of bacon had to be boned ready for slicing, cheeses skinned, and butter cut into slabs and wrapped ready for sale. Mrs. Clarke, herself mother of seven children, listened with a sympathetic ear to her customers' troubles. The whole family was musical, and between them they were proficient on piano, violin, trombone, piccolo and drums. The next window was once a part of a tiny toy shop kept by Miss Gaywood from whom little Ernie Springett bought his first fishing rod and line. It cost him 6d.

13   This particularly charming Spalding picture of 1907 shows David Doe with members of his family outside his home and workplace on the right of the Street. Called Vinehurst, it still stands today opposite the Post Office and is the oldest known example of an inhabited house in the village for, twenty years ago, Vinehurst was dated back to origins of around 1350. Mr. Doe, for twenty-five years a widower, was, within living memory, a boot and shoe-maker and displayed examples of his work in the nearer window. As he worked he whistled 'Sssss sssss' between his teeth. His daughter Minnie sold sweets and minerals from the second part of the shop, over which is displayed the sign *Cyclists Rest*. Thoughts of refreshment must have spurred on many a weary pedaller to gain the top of Hatfield Hill. A straw-hatted driver holds his horse steady outside the Chapel in this scene of a more leisurely age.

14 Standing as it does, at the top of the hill with its spire piercing the skyline, it is easy to spot the Methodist Church. Until 1875, when this, the second church (or chapel) was built for the tendered sum of £797, worshippers gathered in a building directly opposite, now the site of Urban Cottages. Erected beside a pigyard in 1826 this first chapel provided a permanent place of worship and replaced open-air meetings. Mr. George Shelley was an early preacher, while Mr. Joseph Langstone and Mr. William Oliver at one time provided music on the flute and concertina respectively. Local knowledge dictates that, in the Essex earthquake of 1884, the weathercock was toppled from the steeple and was never replaced. It is interesting, therefore, to note that in this Spalding photograph, probably 1907, the weathercock on the steeple appears to be intact. In the First World War the premises were used by the Bedfordshire Yeomanry.

15   Twenty-six men from the village died as a result of the Great War. To commemorate them, and all who served, a Village Hall was erected in 1920 on the site mentioned in card No. 11. The total cost of the hut, building and equipment was £1,000 and the Hall was faced by bricks from Mr. Marriage's brickyard at Nounsley. Concerts, socials, dinners and receptions, whist drives and dances were among events that took place there and are remembered with nostalgia. When the dancing became energetic the wooden floor would bounce and creak sending clouds of dust into the air. The snooker club played at the Hall and it once housed the village library. Heating was by coke-fuelled tortoise stoves which invariably gave off choking fumes when first lit. Necessary additional ventilation was provided by two sliding panels in the roof, opened by a long-handled pole. This couple represent one of many as they emerge from their wedding breakfast.

16   The tiny figure in the middle of the Street in 1907-1908 is Harold Lawrence. His father, James, the youngest of eleven children, was errand boy at Mr. C. Dowsing's shop (now Peverel Estates), whose daughter he married in 1902. In November 1918 the couple bought the business from F. Luckin Smith for £375 and traded there for many years. Cheeses, in 70lb rounds were left to mature for three or four months and sugar was scooped and bagged from a drawer holding one hundredweight. James sold haberdashery, paraffin and ladies' and gents' footwear and did not close until ten o'clock at night. The gentry sent a chauffeur-driven car to collect orders and Mr. Lawrence himself delivered by motor cycle and side car. Recessed, is Mr. Clarke's forge with its paraphernalia set out in front; Forge Cottages follow (now a restaurant) and then the Swan public house. The tree, opposite, marks Church Road corner.

17 At first this scene appears to be the 1930s, but a closer look shows the woman's dress to be ankle length and another card in the series (see No. 46) confirms a date of around 1916. Between Lawrence's shop on the left and Forge Cottages, project the handles of a cart at the Forge itself. In the distance is Springfield House, its long brick wall running down to two cottages built at right angles to the road. Next is Mr. W. Oliver's shop with bakehouse adjacent; a white wooden fence surrounds the garden and a sycamore grows in the grounds near the gap which is Church Road. Mr. Perrin's trade sign stands high in the air beside his three-ga-

bled house appropriately called Gables (see No. 18.) formerly the Golden Lion. Gables and the next three cottages have all been demolished. Urban Cottages with their white fencing are on the extreme right, where a plaque bearing the date of 1895 is just visible on the wall below the roof.

18   Mr. James Perrin's coaching business, the equivalent of today's taxi service, stood at Church Road corner (now the bungalow, Baswin). In 1891 it was the Golden Lion, a beerhouse kept by Isaac Nice. In this card of 1910 Mr. Perrin, complete with top hat and a dustcover across his lap, is seated in the brougham. His commissions ranged from conveying gentry to and from the railway station to taking families to the seaside. The groom, nicknamed 'Pigeon', is surnamed either Guilder or Pannell, and the horse is called Boxer. Another horse, Edward, was commandeered by the Bedfordshire Yeomanry, stationed in the village during the Great War, three officers being billeted with the family. Mrs. Perrin later took in washing and ironing, usual work for many women, hanging out the wet clothes to dry on a line strung between trees in the Garden Field. Pink and white horse chestnut trees (since felled) stand in the background.

19   Mr. Oliver's bakehouse stood at the junction of Church Road and the Street on the site of today's Kitchen Design Centre. The shop and house, seen here, fronted the old Roman road and the replacement building has been aptly named 'Oliver House'. Entry to the shop was by the side door where a brass bell on a coiled spring tinkled on entry. Five generations of Olivers carried on the business, the earliest being born in 1823 and named William, the first of four to bear that name. The last was called Charles. Bread was baked daily, year in, year out, and delivered to the door by horse and cart. In the 1920s, the round extended over a wide area covering Boreham, Little Baddow, Woodham Walter, Ulting and as far as Langford church. Most of this round was amicably shared with another family of bakers, the Cleaves. At Christmas, villagers brought oversized festive fowl to be cooked in the capacious ovens.

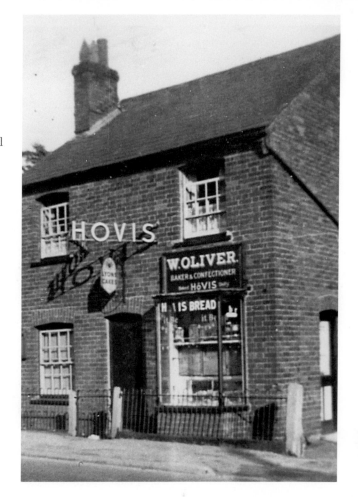

20   Street Farm adjoined the cottages called The Limes and today is the site of Flats 2-12, Swan Close. George Knight, who ran Street Farm, died in 1902 and his wife in 1915, after which their unmarried daughter, Julia, carried on the business. Where today the by-pass runs, cows were kept in a meadow behind the farm and, for the price of one penny, villagers could buy a jug of milk at the door. Miss Knight retired in 1923, selling the business to Mr. George Smith, whose son, Ted, started a milk round using a horse and small cart, ladling the milk by hand out of a churn. With the advent of Lord Rayleigh's Dairies mechanisation, the function of the farm changed to Road House. A round disk on the left positioned next to one of the two original wrought-iron gates leading to the Farm, reads: *Official Quarters National Cyclists' Union.* Deckchairs are set out behind the brick wall in the shade of a horse chestnut in bloom.

21 In this card, franked 1912, we have moved on but a few yards. The rough surface of the road is clearly visible and merges almost imperceptibly into the footpaths. Behind the leafy trees on the left stands the pair of sturdy little early-18th century cottages called The Limes, seen earlier, and looking much the same today. They are opposite the car park entrance, but no lime trees remain. Hatfield Cottage stands on the nearer side of Station Road, where the signpost points its finger firmly towards Terling. From Quince Lodge, on the further side, to the distant Providence Cottage lies open land bounded by wire strands and known simply as 'The Wires'. Football was played here and behind the 'Duke' (see No. 39). To our right the long brick wall of Springfield House comes to an end and, as we now follow the pointing finger to the railway station, nothing stirs in the Street save two small girls.

HATFIELD PEVEREL . 770

22   We have rounded Station Road corner. Two lath and plaster cottages, similar in style to those seen in card No. 11, and possibly once an inn or beerhouse, stand to our left. In 1930 Mr. Walter Peirce moved into the nearer of the pair reversing his horse-drawn cart into the window of the house next door! The terrace of four brick houses whose front doors opened into a passage leading straight through to the back, stood on the site of the recently-erected house at No. 1, Station Road. On fine summer evenings the inhabitants brought out chairs placed directly beside the road to sit and watch the world go by. It was known locally as 'Hell's Row' because of the loud arguments between certain of the occupiers. In a yard at the back, Mr. George Pease, inhabitant, and coalman for Moy's, kept his open-topped cart, and horse. The steam engine used for road mending and watering, together with its green painted cart, was also kept here.

23　As early as 1843 Hatfield Peverel had a railway station. Six years later it was totally destroyed by fire, and it was not until 1st March 1878 that a new station was opened by the Great Eastern Railway Company. The outward appearance has changed little enough to be instantly recognizable in this postcard dated 1915. Two exceptions are the signal box, its roof barely visible on the extreme left, and the covered, wooden footbridge where passengers crossed to the down-line to Colchester. A plan of the station in 1909 gives evidence of a far larger complex, showing sidings, goods yard and coal yard, as well as the gardens apportioned to the stationmaster, signalmen and platelayers. Today the rough surfaces of the goods yard and the forecourt, the latter seen here, have been tarmacked and are in use as car parks. In 1994 the station won the award of *Best Small Station* in this region. The '1850' is a reference number, not a date.

1850.　G.E.R. Station, Hatfield Peverel.

Fred Spalding Photo. Chelmsford. Copyright

24   A view of the down line in 1915 is seen through the arch of the beautifully-designed footbridge. Spanning the track its steps are of wood and a canopy covers passengers as they transfer from one platform to the other. The signal box, also a wooden structure, was manned by signalmen working shifts, and certain late night travellers were often invited in for a 'fry-up' of eggs and bacon cooked on a gleaming shovel over the hot tortoise stove! At one time manned by a staff of around 26 the station also had a large and thriving goods yard, now the area covered by the larger car park. On both platforms freight awaits despatch or collection.

The scalloped, roofed shelter on the left with its very low seat has only recently been dismantled and replaced. Tilley oil lamps lit the platforms, an open lock-up kiosk displays its wares and Lord Rayleigh's Dairies sign can be seen in the station yard.

G.E. RAILWAY STATION, HATFIELD PEVEREL. 1851.

Fred Spalding
Photo
Chelmsford
Copyright

25 In the first decade of the 1900s Lord Rayleigh's Dairies Refrigerating Station was built as a collecting depot and cooling plant. Milk from nearby farms was brought here and the milk cooled before being poured into churns and loaded on to the trains. Much of the milk came from Terling and for the horse pictured here the haul up Station Hill must have been hard work. The plant, shown here and in the preceding picture, is marked on a G.E.R. station plan dated 28th January 1909, and is situated opposite the booking hall entrance. Simply marked 'Dairy', a pencilled note adds: *Rayleigh pays £2.2s (two guineas) per year for use of Yard*. The plan also shows a rough sketch, marking a proposed additional building, on the present site. How that building has grown! In the late 1930s the Station Yard plant was closed and converted into two cottages, their front gardens still standing unusually high.

26   As we turn to retrace our steps to the Street, we pass this 1927 view of two buildings at the left of the station exit: the Temperance Hotel and Yew Tree Cottage. In the census of 1891 Daniel Death, aged 60, lived at the cottage and his occupation is given as: *Cat, Rat and Mice Destroyer!* Seen here with its roof thatched, the house is marked on a map of 1897 as the only building on that side of Station Road. It is also known to have been the school which young Horace Moore (born 1873) attended, as later did his granddaughter, Mrs. Hilary Doe (Cable). The Temperance Hotel, popular with cycling clubs and local inhabitants, was entered by the door on the left where customers sat on hard, wooden settle-type seats. Cakes, covered by round, glass domes, were set out in tempting array on the long counter and soft drinks only were sold. In the 1920s Mrs. Alice Wicks ran the hotel and her sister, Miss Annie Isted, the school.

27   Still in Station Road we approach the signpost seen in No. 21. Behind the uniformed bandsman lies the Street with the tall chimneys of Springfield House stable block to our right. Facing us is the ivy-covered house, Wisteria Cottage, once owned by Mr. E. Ward, saddler and harness maker (established 1850). In a Parish Magazine of 1908 he advertises: *Portmanteaux and Trunks made and repaired on the premises. Every Stable requisite supplied.* He made leather footballs for the club and one of his men, Mr. George Lucking, made Ernie Springett a wrist strap, still good today. Miss Julia Knight later retired here from Street Farm (see No. 20), after which it became Mrs. Lyne's draper's shop (see No. 8) and until recently it was a bookshop. It now stands empty. To its left are two of the terrace of four brick cottages which appear in a sale catalogue of 1922 and which were sold for £400 the lot!

28   Little Horace (Horrie) Moore (see No. 26) grew into an enterprising man. Born in 1873, the son of Cornelius Moore, baker and postmaster, he later lived at No. 3, The Terrace, working as a postman and cycle repairer. In 1899, from a shed at his home, he advertised his business as: *Motor Cycles & Cycles, Pram Repairs*, and when, in 1914, he moved to Quince Lodge in the Street he took the shed with him. Seen here beside his garage in Station Road (now Marshall's) he sits astride the motor cycle with side car which he made in 1920. He sold petrol in two-gallon drums, delivering them on his machine. Mr. Moore was an accomplished trumpeter, and, in contrast with his casual appearance here, was photographed by Fred Spalding wearing the splendid apparel (complete with top hat) of official trumpeter at the opening of the Chelmsford Assize. The business closed in April 1992 and the 'shed' is now occupied by Martin Phillips, stationer.

29 We have moved on in time to 1928, the year this card was posted. In 1921 the rough road surface of the Street was macadamised and the pavements kerbed. Our pedestrian does not pause as he takes a step to cross Station Road, while the driver of the solitary car steers blithely along the very centre of the road. The signpost, now moved to the other side of the Street (see No. 21) lies in the shadow of the house on this sunny summer morning, and by enlargement it has been possible to decipher the lettering. It reads: *Hatfield Station, Terling, Leighs, Felste(a)d and Dunmow*. Few today would choose to take this slow and tortuous route to reach the final destination. Mr. F. Ower's creeper-covered house with its business premises stands to the right and is now Scott's Restaurant. Next is Peppercorn, with The Limes and Street Farm hidden behind trees; the Swan Inn is just visible at the far end of the Street.

HATFIELD PEVEREL

30   About 1898 Mr. Charles Watson had his building business (see No. 48) in the Street. Twenty years on, in 1918, and near the same spot, a young Albert Cable poses nonchalantly with others in front of the large quince tree which gave its name to Quince Lodge and Cottage; the roof of Horace Moore's 'shed' adjoins. Road widening in 1953 reduced the depth of the front gardens by six feet. The bigger break in the wall on the right is Station Road, while in the house immediately beyond, now Scott's Restaurant, once lived Mr. F. Owers, the village undertaker. The brick house just discernible on the extreme left is one of the terrace of four (see No. 27), with Wisteria Cottage and the stable house of Springfield House adjoining. This large house has since been demolished but stood on the site of the car park and Hadfelda Square. In front of the light cart, also on the left, a man with his bicycle turns the wheel to cross the road.

The Street Hatfield Peverel.

31   In the early 1920s Mr. Edward Claydon set up the Universal Garage in the Street. Intriguing advertisements appear in both windows and the one on the left is still fitted with the original glass. Today the garage belongs to the Coward family and the triangular-shaped roof now has an identical twin extending as far as the gateway on the right. This gateway, still there, once gave access to White Hart Cottage in Maldon Road. Behind the fence is a field of standing corn where Mr. Ernie Wright remembers once picking peas. Today, Redman & Hales, the Milestone Estate and part of St. Andrew's Road occupy the site while the spinney of elm trees once grew at the junction of Bennett Way and the footpath to Toulmin Road. On the forecourt stand three splendid vehicles identified as a Matchless Model H motorcycle combination with a spring frame; a motorcycle, possibly a B.S.A.; and what is probably a three-wheeler Morgan Runabout.

32   This postcard of the Street, dated August 1925, should be viewed with the card that follows. We are outside Chestnut Cottages and look back towards Station Road. On the right is the wooden building earlier owned by coachbuilder, Fred Diaper, but here by two brothers, Frank and Dick Bright, wheelwright and coachbuilder, respectively. Today it is the premises of a dentist and a central heating business while the house in which Frank's family lived is a florist's shop. Next door, Mr. Louis Cleave succeeded Cornelius Moore who was both baker and postmaster, the latter occupation being carried on in the room with the bay window (now a pizza take-away). The low-roofed, wooden-walled building is the flour shed (tyre centre) and in the road stands Mr. Cleave's Model T Ford van. Providence Cottage, the home of Mr. Henry Wood, green-grocer and market gardener, is now a betting agency and the Mace Stores occupy the site of his small wooden shop.

33   From the flour-mixing shed of Cleave's on our left, we look along the neat fencing to the sign of the Duke of Wellington public house. In this card, which probably pre-dates 1914, the side door of the house leads into the bakery, the bay window is the old post office and roses scramble up the wall of Mr. Frank Bright's home. Brothers Frank and Richard (Dick) Bright carried on their combined business of wheelwright and coachmaker in the tall, white building. Carts were made on the upper floor and sent down on inclined planks while wheels were wrought below. After the war Dick began to build a bus. The advertisement on the huge, partly thatched, barn, reads: *Dunlop Tyre Stock*, while inside, farming tackle was stored, Mr. Wood threshed grain and children played. With a forge situated across the road it was an ideal spot for soldiers to bed down with their horses. Since demolished, it is now the site of the Wellington car park.

34   This is the bus that Dick Bright built. The engine was a Ford Model T and the wooden body was painted dark red; Dick completed it just in time to take a party to the first Cup Final to be held at Wembley in 1923. A bench ran on either side, passengers facing, and twice-daily on Fridays he transported women to Chelmsford market for a fare of one shilling return. They chattered all the way there and back and it became known as 'The Parrot Cage'. Other expeditions included Bank Holiday trips to Maldon, ferrying darts teams to matches at Maldon and Southend, and taking pupils from Hatfield Peverel and Terling schools to Witham for woodwork and cookery classes. With seats removed, Dick carried dead pigs to Southend and helped with house moving. Three other members of the Bright family, Harold, Alfred and Norman, appear in this photograph of the local darts team on an outing to Epping, and Dick, himself, is on the far left.

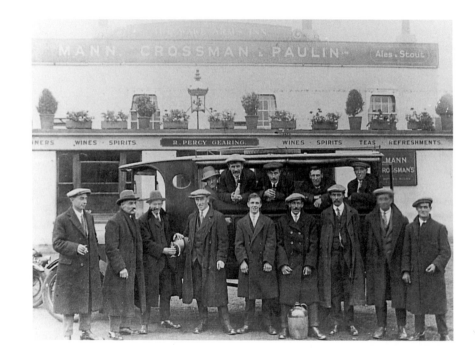

35 We now move to the Duke sign and look back across the road to Blacksmith's Yard, today part of the Tyre Centre. At the Forge, the roof of which is seen sandwiched between the two groups of houses, Henry Harris, blacksmith, carried on the trade of his father, Joseph. Henry's own son, William, who worked with him, served as a farrier with the Royal Horse Artillery in the Great War. In the Parish Magazine of February 1917 he, and several other serving men, are mentioned as having received letters and parcels from home. To our left are Chestnut Cottages, a terrace of three built in 1865. A group of seven children stand outside the gate of No. 1. and possibly include some of Mr. E. Wright's family who at the time lived in No. 2. The author, herself, was later born at No. 3. It is interesting to note that even at a time of little motorised traffic the brick wall outside this last house has been partially knocked down.

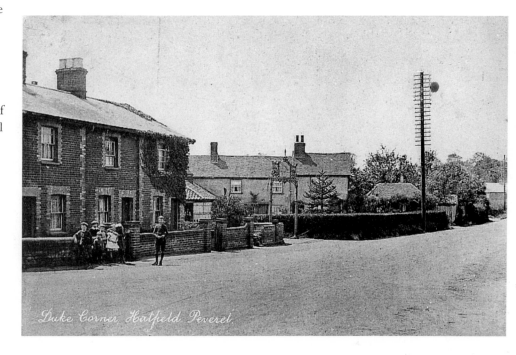

Duke Corner Hatfield Peverel.

36   Ethel Harris's occupation as the only woman blacksmith in the country was of sufficient interest for this photograph to appear in a national newspaper during the First World War and certainly worthy of inclusion in our book. Born in 1879, she was the only daughter of Mr. Henry Harris and his wife. By 1891, Henry was a widower and Ethel not only helped bring up the family, but also assisted in the forge. Henry himself died in 1916 and Ethel, a familiar figure in a leather apron, worked full-time as farrier. Upon her skills, many soldiers depended to keep their horses well shod. Here, in front of one of the two fires at the forge, and fashioning a harrow, she wields a fearsome-looking and heavy, seven-pound hammer. In 1924 Ethel married Fred Brett and they converted the small building seen next the road in the previous and following cards into a garage. William, her brother, returned from Rutland to take over the forge.

37　In a directory of 1882 Henry Harris is listed as one of two blacksmiths, a trade he was to follow for more than thirty years. Framed by the magnificent wrought-iron-work sign he made with William, his son, we see Henry standing outside the door of his forge around the year 1910. The sign, which reads: *H. Harris Farrier & General Smith* was later sold by his daughter, Ethel, and shipped to America, but William's weather-vane remains. The old house was shared by three families, the Harris family occupying the largest part on the right. Today it is one cottage, Salvadore, and two flats called Hooks and Sheaves. Sharp eyes will spot the workmen, among them two of Henry's sons, with another, Fred, on the right and nattily attired in plus-fours. In the First World War, army horses and mules packed the yard waiting to be shod and branded. In 1924 the small building near the road was converted by Mr. Fred Brett, Ethel's husband, to become the Forge Garage.

38   Standing at a prime spot on the old coaching road from London to Norwich and opposite Maldon Road, is The Duke of Wellington public house. It was first listed as a pub in 1832 when it was kept by Sarah Edwards and still offers refreshment for weary travellers, although today's coaches are motorised. D. Mills was landlord from 1902 to 1912 and his name appears here on the main sign. The projecting board reads: *Cyclists & Parties, Dinners & Teas Provided* and the one below: *Pratt's Spirits*. As horse and cart await the driver's emergence from the hostelry, a young man stares down at the ground and a bearded gent strides out towards home. Note the light trap standing near the fence. Right beside the road are the small, brick-built Feoffee almshouses with further chimneys visible near the tree. In the distance is the Terrace (see No. 40), where today's slip road makes its hazardous entry on to the A12 bypass.

THE DUKE CORNER,
HATFIELD PEVEREL.

39   The football team of 1904, shorts supported by belts or neckties, poses outside the Wellington pub. Standing centrally is D. Mills, landlord, with far right, Ernie Wright; seated bottom left is Arthur Ashby. Now a Ridley's house, it was then owned by Brown's Brewery on the Green. *The Official Handbook of the Cricket, Cycling, Football & Athletic Clubs of Essex* for 1907, lists the club's colours as light and dark blue with its headquarters, dressing room and ground at the Duke of Wellington. It had forty members and the cricket club thirty-five, both clubs playing at the same venue. Football was later played behind Shepherd's Cottage in Church Road, then on ground opposite Station Road donated in 1926 by Mr. N. de Bond of Springfield House. Today, matches take place on the recreation ground (given by the Strutt family) with proposed plans for three pitches in the Wickham Bishops Road. Cricket is played in Church Road (see No. 60).

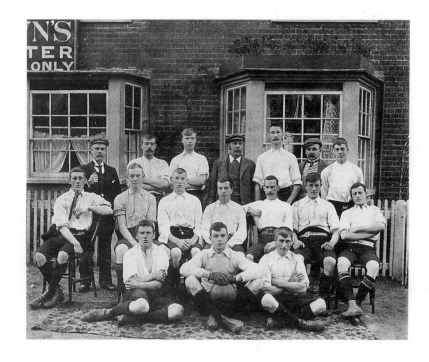

40   Beyond the Wellington pub stretches the road to Witham and we stand outside the ten terraced homes which were built in 1881. Their light-coloured bricks came from the brickfield, once owned by Mr. Clover, which lay directly behind the houses. Mr. E. Springett, now 96, recalls that his father, Josiah, worked there. In this card of 1925 Mr. Walter Scrivener sells flowers from his bungalow garden, a spot where none today would stop to buy. It stands close to the notoriously-dangerous slip road on to the A12 bypass. Behind the hedge, opposite, Mr. Edgar Nettleton of Bovingtons Farm planted orchards of apples, plums, gages, pears and cherries, and fields of soft fruit, on land that stretched to the Wickham Bishops Road. Women pickers recall passing plums over the hedge to soldiers of the Great War, convalescing at Bridge Hospital in Witham and out for a walk. In 1994 'Smallacres', the last remnant of this fruit-picking area, closed.

41   We have returned to the Wellington public house yard where we stand looking at the signpost pointing to Maldon Road. The date is around 1916 and in the foreground on the left is the side of the newly-erected Nurse's Home. Beyond the Home a white sheet flaps on a linen line in the back garden of what is probably the house now called Stuarts and an elm tree stands silhouetted against the sky. To the right of the picture stand two more of the brick-walled Chestnut Cottages (now Ash Close) which may have taken their name from the chestnut trees, then in the grounds of Tudor Lodge, and which still grow opposite. Beyond is the small shop kept for many years by the Turpin family (see No. 43), while behind the distant picket fence are the two houses known as Kimberley Cottages. The last house is Pretoria. There were then no further homes on the right until just before the Parish Room.

42   A stone tablet set into the wall of the bungalow, aptly-named 'Nightingales' and now a private dwelling, reads: *Parish Nurse's Home erected by Walter Butler Esq., & presented to the parish 1912-1919.* A Nursing Association had been started in the village in 1904 when the nurse's yearly salary was £32 2s. 6d. and lodging allowance set at £11 3s. 0d. In October 1908 her fees for attending a patient were 1d. a visit or 6d. per week. Three of the early parish, or district nurses, were nurses Cook, Hutchinson and Biggs. In this self-written postcard, District Nurse Rita Glanfield stands at the door of the Home. She took up her post here in November 1930 and her daughter, Ilma, then a small girl, remembers that a concrete path was being laid to the front door in which she left a footprint. The path has since been replaced by slabs. Many people who still live in the village today were delivered by one of the nurses named above.

43　The recently-erected house called Tanfield, near Ash Close in the Maldon Road, stands on the site of Mr. Harold Lawrence's electrical shop, later Dr. Emerick's surgery. Directory entries spanning 1839-1899 show the shop, seen here behind an attractive picket fence, to have been occupied by a family called Turpin, the name displayed over the door in this photograph, possibly of 1899. Thomas Turpin, shopkeeper and grocer in 1839, was succeeded by Mrs. Ann Turpin, his widow, and then by Miss Kezia Turpin, their daughter. In 1891, aged 69, Kezia is described as 'grocer and draper' and we know that she sold sweets, some costing as little as a farthing and which she weighed out on scales. Miss Ellen Lawrence, only sister of James (see No. 16), next had the business, and she too sold sweets. Liquorice allsorts, shoelaces, chocolate drops, treacle dabs, coconut haystacks, bullseyes and aniseed balls were there for the choosing.

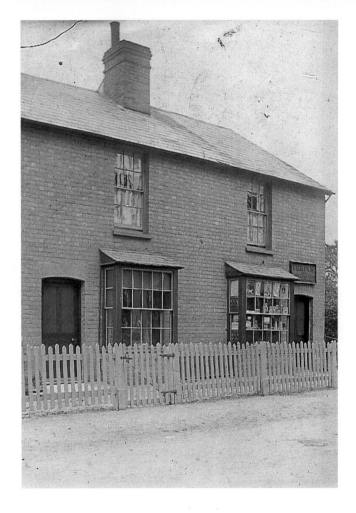

44   Langford Cottages occupied the site in Maldon Road where Stuarts stands today; during restoration in 1938 the date 1643 was found marked on a beam in the attic. In 1915, about the date of this card, it was occupied by the Crow, Bright and Wallace families, the last-named family gaining access through a door at the back. The bow window marks an earlier Post Office as shown on a map of 1876 and as recounted by Mrs. Crow to Miss N. May. Inside, a long counter ran from front to back and customers entered through the nearby door. Mr. Tom Crow and Mr. David Wright of the Wellington pub each owned a very fast pony and a light cart. Jim Reeves of Chelmsford joined them in a pony and cart three-horse race along the old A12, starting at the Black Boy (now Menzies shop) in Springfield Road and ending at the Duke. It is not known who won! Soldiers stabled their horses in sheds seen at the rear on the right.

45 White Hart Cottage, built about 1520 on the edge of common land in Maldon Road, was for at least three hundred years an inn or beerhouse. Francis Marchante of Hatfield Peverel was indicted for 'an annoyance' at the Chelmsford Quarter Sessions where it was recorded that: on 1 January 1606-7... *he kept a common inn at Hatfield Peverel called the White Hart... and that the said inn had been a common inn from time out of mind...* What the 'annoyance' was we do not know. In March 1906, it was sold for £1,650 and described as: *a free beerhouse, having a licence to sell and consume on the premises, with adjoining cottage and gardens.* Taken early in this century, the photograph shows an unidentified family in the front garden with open countryside beyond the porch. Mr. Arthur Bennett, by 1895 village school headmaster, later made this his home and brought boys from school to help dig his garden as part of their lessons (see No. 50).

46   We have moved a few yards along the Maldon Road. On this card, dated 5th May 1916, the bungalow roof on the far left pinpoints Roseglen and beyond is the chimney of the Nurse's Home. At right angles to the road are Cheshunt Cottage and Garden Cottage, both much the same today. Langford Cottages, seen in card No. 44, come next. Little Mabel Wallace lived here, staying safely behind her fence as sheep and cattle on their way to market filled the road from side to side, urged on by the sticks and loud shouts of the drovers. When she and her brother Bob caught scarlet fever, they were taken from here to Braintree hospital by horse-drawn ambulance. Two lath and plaster cottages, since demolished, complete the picture. On the left lived Bill and Emma Pease while in the further right lived Miss Langstone, an expert needlewoman. The wooden fences and gates of these two cottages remain and can still be seen today.

47   Overcrowding and insanitary conditions marked some of the older houses on the Green, in the Street and Station Road as being unfit for human habitation. In 1921 Braintree Council began building houses, the first ones being on the Green. Bricks came from Mr. Marriage's brickyard at Nounsley, where Mr. Tom Carrington and Mr. Charles Harrington (among others) worked under foreman Mr. Dan. Pennock. This postcard of around 1930 shows the Council houses in New Road shortly after the first part was completed in 1927 and when it could truly be described as 'new'. With number 24 on our left we stand near the entry to Wood-field Way and look towards Maldon Road. Under the noonday sun, windows of the brand-new houses have been flung open, gardens have just begun to be cultivated and children are out at play. Beyond Maldon Road, where shops now stand, lies open ground and the Old School playing field, still remembered by many.

NEW RD. HATFIELD PEVERELL

48   Older residents may recognise this peaceful scene of around 1905 as the busy road to Maldon. Pulling its cart, a horse comes into view on the left close to a stile in the hedge, while the trees on the right grow near the modern Village Hall. A small girl and a woman, bonneted against the sun, walk in front of a row of terraced cottages; in one of these at a later date lived Mr. Walter Hume, boot repairer. Woman and child approach the first gated entrance to the Vicarage (Woodham Drive), where a gravelled driveway curved round in front of the large house. It emerged opposite the distant Parish Room, now the Salvation Army Headquarters. By the second gate grew a magnificent beech with other mature trees and shrubbery lining the roadside. The Parish Room was built by Mr. Charles Watson in 1895 at a cost of £547, towards which William Tufnell Esq. of Hatfield Place gave £200, the remainder being raised by public subscription.

49   Still around 1905, and from outside the Parish Room, Spalding shows us a further peaceful scene looking toward the Wheatsheaf corner. On the left are the Lovibond almshouses or *Monied Housen*, founded in 1820 by Martha Lovibond. Next is the Old School, built in 1851. Its large window, still paned with glass and part of the master's house, overlooks the boys' yard. No doubt this window took the full force of balls and stones kicked up from the rough surface of the yard for it was later blocked in. An elm grows inside the school gate, an oak in the corner of the yard and a second oak, still surviving, grows in an almshouse garden. The distant house is Ann Cottage, one of a terrace of three dating back to the 1600s, with Mr. Drury, possibly the parish letter writer, living next door at Grange Cottage around 1850. Shrubbery stretches back to the Parish Room, intersected only by Church Road.

Hatfield

Fred Spalding
Photo Chelmsford
Copyright

50 Armed with an awesome array of gardening implements, this group of young lads pose, in 1919, in the boys' yard with Mr. Arthur Bennett, a respected headmaster. Nicknamed 'Billy' by the boys, he is seated centre on a wheelbarrow, surrounded by boys bearing spades, forks, hoes, rakes, a pickaxe, a bagging hook and a bucket. Gardening formed an important part of their education, this plot of land becoming, later, the site of the canteen. The school held an allotment behind Brewery House on the Green (see No. 66) and when Mr. Bennett moved to White Hart Cottage (see No. 45) the boys dug the garden. All these boys are known but space permits naming only one: fifth from right is George Sadler. In the background stand Redlynch Cottages, the further, 15th century wooden dwellings, since demolished; the later, brick-built ones since restored. Beyond the washing strung out on the line are the chimneys of the Old Vicarage.

51   On a sleepy summer's afternoon in 1907 the Old School basks in warm sunshine. Maldon Road lies empty, save for a solitary pedestrian and a wagonette pulled up against the hedge opposite the almshouses. The school, built in 1851 to accommodate two hundred children, and with walls 14 inches thick, was several times enlarged. In the little tower at the front hangs the bell that called the children to their lessons. Railings, and a long wooden fence which stretches from the brick pillar in front of the building to the extreme right, mark off the playground from the pavement. A small gate in the fence seems unused as the sprouting grass is untrodden. Few will remember the tall elm tree that grew outside the boys' porch and today only the railings remain as evidence of this much-loved old building. It was demolished in 1991 and is now a Shaftesbury housing complex suitably named Old School Court.

THE SCHOOLS, HATFIELD PEVEREL.   H Hall, Photo, Witham

52   Still in 1907 we now make a diversion to wend our way along Church Road. There are no footpaths so we stand in the road to look back at the Old School. On the left is the Master's house with its ivy-covered walls and, almost hidden from sight on the right is the high, pointed window of the classroom seen beneath the bell tower in the preceding card. In 1923 Mr. Sidney Hiscock succeeded Mr. Bennett and Miss Lucy Croxall became his assistant. On either side of us extends the leafy growth which has always been known in the village as the 'Shrub'. It was indeed, just that, and was once part of common land which stretched from the Green to the Street. Today, on the right, the house called Kissingate stands at the road junction with Maldon Road, while on the larger portion of shrubland to the left stands a small housing estate, The Spinney, built around 1967. Here, beside a pond, there once grew violets, celandines and primroses.

HATFIELD PEVEREL 436.

Fred Spalding.
Photo.
Chelmsford.
Copyright.

53   Time has moved on to around 1930, but we remain at the spot seen in the last card, merely turning our heads to look right. For generations of children the 'Shrub', where hornbeams bordered the road, provided an exciting out-of-school playground. Hide-and-seek and kiss-and-tell (or not to tell!) were played here, while many an illicit Woodbine was puffed behind a tree. Warm summer days would often find pupils and teacher engaged here in lessons: reading, needlework or physical training. On one occasion the shrubs provided shelter for a truant as he lay in ambush for the headmaster – the miscreant was caught and severely caned. Through the trees, and beyond a little cut, we see the white walls of Shrub Cottage on the right and Peverel Cottage on the left, while the solid chimney of one of three ancient houses can be seen further left. For many years the Scouts and Guides had their headquarters in a hut in this clearing in the 'Shrub'.

THE SHRUBBERY, HATFIELD PEVEREL

54   To capture a well-proportioned photograph of St. Andrew's Priory Church is not easy for it lacks its tower and transepts, burned down in 1231, and has had aisles added. Here, around 1906, Fred Spalding found what is probably the best viewpoint. The cross on the roof above the rounded Norman arch marks the east of the present church and the west end of the former tower. In 1875, extensive repairs closed the church for worship and on 30th May the vicar wrote in the register: ... *a stone coffin was found with bones of a man and a woman at the foot of the wall between the window containing the effigy of Ingelrica and the last window to the east...* A legend runs that the devil said he would have Ingelrica's soul whether she be buried inside or outside the church, so within the walls themselves may have provided a solution. In 1923, Mr. Alfred J. Steele, a local man, published a comprehensive history of the earlier priory and the church.

55 At the far eastern end is the rounded Norman arch which, before a disastrous fire in 1231, was part of the west end of the square tower. On either side of this arch, now above the altar, can be seen the illuminated texts so beloved by the Victorians and filling the space above is an illustration of the Lord, surrounded by angels. The wall is now bare. To the left is the north aisle, the three complete arches dating back to about 1280, while in the space above the column joining the further two arches is a splayed Norman window of around 1080-1100. It formed part of the original exterior wall and, being narrow on the outside and wider on the inside, it kept out rain and cold while letting in maximum light. On the furthermost window sill lies the effigy mentioned in the last card and supposed to be Ingelrica. Through the arches on the right is the south aisle, once part of the priory. The church is lit by lamps and candles.

56   Of the several postcard views of Hatfield Priory, including those taken by Spalding, perhaps this one published by F. Baker around 1920 most pleases the eye. It is of the west side of the house, which from 1768 until 1928 was owned by John Wright and his descendants. Here a herd of black and white Friesians peacefully graze within the grounds. In February 1898 Christopher W. Parker, D.L., J.P., then resident here, penned a letter to Edward Fitch, an Essex County Councillor. Addressed from Hatfield Priory, Witham, he wrote: … *I came home yesterday after riding a bicycle from Shenfield to Ongar and then to Chelmsford grumbling much…* Between Kelvedon Hatch and Ongar, then Ongar to Norton Heath he found the road to be in a very bad state and in need of attention. He concludes: …*I should say L. Marriage has been carting grain all the winter and there is a great cause of the mischief.*

The Priory Hatfield Peverel

57   Retracing our steps from the private drive of the Priory, we pass the Church on our right to arrive in front of the four brick pillars which mark the entrance to both buildings. The most striking feature of this view is the wealth of trees. From this spot and back to the Shrubbery, Church Road was overhung on either side by a canopy of horse chestnuts. To the right stands Priory Lodge, very old and once the vicarage, being partly destroyed by fire in 1916. Today the drive has been widened and two gates have disappeared. Surprisingly perhaps, it appears that the wheels of cars have rutted the gravel drive more than those of the horse-drawn carriages of yesteryear. To our left lies Priory Park, into which, in the First World War a Zeppelin in distress jettisoned its tools, quickly seized upon by villagers watching its slow progression overhead. Once outside the gates we turn left and continue along Church Road.

Priory Lodge, Hatfield Peverel

58   A lens reveals Shepherd's Cottage beyond the distant figure and pinpoints this location in Church Road. In a summer scene of around 1930 the picture's charm lies in the dappled shadows cast by a profusion of trees, making Church Road a popular place for a gentle Sunday stroll. Unpaved, and bordered by sheep's parsley, wild flowers spring from the grass growing lush on either side. To our right is the field known as Willermer Downs where, in the 1890s, Mr. John Upson, farmer, once fenced-in overnight about thirty donkeys. The local children seized the opportunity to ride them bareback round the field! Here there grew several horse chestnuts and, in autumn, the children would throw up cudgels to bring down the shiny, ripe conkers. A patch of parsley marks the church end of the long curve of Willow Crescent which emerges opposite Shepherd's Cottage. Land to the left of the road belongs to the Priory.

59   We have arrived outside the cottage only faintly visible in the last picture, and here, in around 1910, the only house in Church Road. It was to remain so for almost another forty years. In the 1890s twelve people lived at Shepherd's Cottage: Samuel Drury, his wife Mary Ann and their ten children. At the gate, in this remarkably sharp photograph, are Mary Ann and her daughter, Kate, who was born in 1877. Two of her sons stand outside the door with the porch. Customers entered by this door to buy the sweets which Mrs. Drury obtained from Hawkes Bros. of Chelmsford and villagers still remember her taking the sweets round to sell to work-ers in the fields. In the cricket season she prepared the teas for players on their ground adjoining. Both Mary Ann's father, and her husband, Samuel, worked as carpenters on the Priory Estate. Much al-tered, it still retains the name of Shepherd's Cottage.

60   This elegantly-attired wedding group of 1902 was seen on television in 1958, when the bride appeared with Eammon Andrews as the subject of the programme: *This is Your Life*. From Shepherd's Cottage, Mary Ann Drury prepared the teas for the cricket club, so what more natural than she should organize the wedding breakfast in the pavilion there for her daughter, Minnie? Olive Prior, four years old and Minnie's niece, was the tiny bridesmaid pictured here outside the old pavilion which blew down last year. Minnie, a tomboy who rode donkeys bare-back, went into service at ten years old. In 1888, on an impulse and aged just sixteen, she took a single-fare train ticket to Paris where she found herself work. She came home to marry. In her life she met many famous people such as Colonel Cody and Annie Oakley; she took a guest house; acted in films; and became dresser to Jessie Matthews, Kay Cavendish and Alicia Markova.

61 We are standing at the Church Road junction with Crabbs Hill about 1930, looking back at a scene familiar to generations of villagers. Shepherd's Cottage is this time viewed from the direction of the Street. On the left in the foreground is the little kissing-gate from which ran a footpath to emerge in Maldon Road. Only part of the path remains, starting now from the top of Baker Avenue while the entrance to this road is in the area of the two tall poles. The ditched field next the gate was farmed by Mr. Claude Galliphant, who at one time kept his pigs here. Behind the dense foliage on the right is the cricket field and it was then the ambition of all batsmen to hit a six clear out of the ground, over the road, and into the pig yard! The fence in the foreground is on the corner of Crabbs Hill, while that on the right of Church Road, near the approaching man, contains a wooden gate which is still there today.

CHURCH ROAD, HATFIELD PEVEREL

62   Back once more in Maldon Road, we leave the school behind to stand on the blind bend outside the Wheatsheaf pub. Here, in 1922, this group of eight young lads, among them George Sadler, pose unconcerned in the very centre of the road, which today is busy with traffic. The small girl seems camera-shy. On the left is the white fence of the Wheatsheaf beer garden where the brick wall, still partly intact, now leads to the car park. Next stand two houses, since demolished, the larger being Langleys, built in the 17th century and once the home of Mrs. Ketley. Her niece recalls that it had a door with a particularly draughty keyhole. Should any of the family suffer from a sty on the eye her aunt advocated pressing the eye against the hole. Apparently it did the trick! Fred Baker's stores (from where this card was bought) and the roof of two old cottages can be seen behind the bunch of boys. On the right stands Ann Cottage.

HATFIELD PEVEREL 1922

63   Mr. Fred Baker opened 'The People's Store', on the Green around 1900. This card, posted 4th June 1907, clearly defines his property with its advertisement on the wall of his house. He sold all that villagers required whether it be bacon, butter or boot-laces, or galvanized pails which hung from hooks on the ceiling. Some of our post-cards came from his shop. The white-fronted house in the centre of the scene is the Wheatsheaf beerhouse with its pleasant, fenced lawn shaded by a 'Brown Brewer' pear tree. The landlord, Mr. Cullum, kept an Airedale dog which allowed small children to ride on its back. The nearer cottages on the left still stand, but the further pair, known as far back as 1725 as 'Hosiers' have been rebuilt as 'Rose-wood'. Ann Cottage, reputed to be haunted, and once the home of Tommy Spearman, shoemender, has its gable end to the road. Five children pose on the grass for Mr. Af-ford, the photographer.

The Green, Hatfield Peverel.

64   In May 1927 Fred Baker's shop became Branch No. 2. of the Witham Co-operative Society. This old photo shows the shopfront and storerooms. A ladder was used to reach the upper door on the left, behind which, when the business changed hands, assistants Esther Searles and Dorothy Turnage recall finding a room packed with candles, oil-lamp glasses and china pudding basins. The basins were soon snapped up when Mr. King, the manager, offered them at three for one shilling: one each of large, medium and small. Walter (Wally) Curtis was errand boy, delivering big boxes of groceries and cans of paraffin on his trade bike. Galvanized tin baths and wickerwork laundry baskets stand outside and C.W.S. goods fill the window. Posters advertise the services and activities of the Society. The Co-op 'divi' was an unknown factor to young shopper Arthur Britton (later manager) and when asked for his mother's number he gave the number of his house!

65 This view of the Green around 1920 shows the greensward as it was then and much as it remains today. A map of 1777 shows common land or 'green' stretching on either side of the road from this spot right up to the Duke of Wellington corner. Some of the old houses (see Nos. 44-46) mark the boundaries. Within living memory, flocks of sheep on their way to or from Chelmsford market were grazed overnight on the Green. On the extreme right is one of several cottages which have been demolished, while the small walnut tree, today fully grown, marks the garden of Marneys. From 1904 until 1920 the adjoining cottages, now a modern house called Greenaways, were the headquarters of the Salvation Army. This is another card from Mr. Baker's shop (Co-op Villas) outside which a single lime tree still survives today. The distant long, low roof is the Old School while houses on the left and Brewery House wall complete the curve.

The Green Hatfield Peverel

66   The magnificent Brewery chimneys that once towered over the Green are no more, for they were demolished some time after 1927. In 1880 the Hatfield Peverel Brewery belonged to Edwin Rust and Company and was run by Alfred Rust. In 1884 it was sold to Mr. Charles Brown, owner of the maltings in Maltings Lane, Witham. Ian Peaty in his book, *Essex Brewers* writes: … *The premises consisted of a cellar 45 feet x 15 feet, a tun room, 15 feet x 15 feet, fermenting room on the first floor and the brewing room on the second floor. The liquor cistern held six quarters, the malt store was 72 feet x 22 feet on the first floor. The Malthouse was of the 'Kentish' pattern, rotating cowl. There was a 50 feet long drying shed with W.C. and a* 68 *feet long stable block with three horse stalls…* Brewery House, on the extreme left, still dominates the Green, while the building behind the two-horse dray is now a house called Brewery Barn.

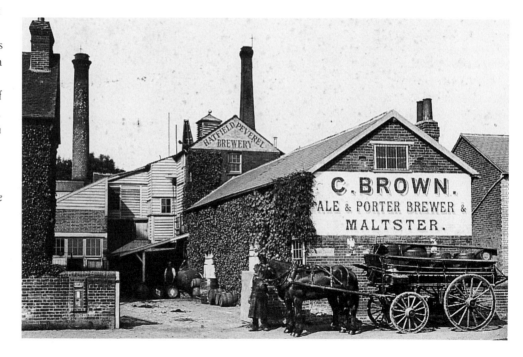

67   The photographer has carefully arranged this group in the Brewery yard. Wearing leather boots and aprons, probably made in the village, these sturdy-looking men needed all their strength. Rolling big barrels of beer and humping heavy crates such as those seen here, was no job for a weakling. On the left, the man with the horse and dray is the carter. Four other Brewery workers pose near the barrels, the bowler hat possibly denoting the wearer's position as head brewer. Behind the boxes, the man sporting collar and tie could be a buyer or seller while the splendidly turned out gent leaning against the wall may well be Mr. Charles Brown himself. In *Durrant's Essex Guide* of 1887, a pictorial advertisement gives Rust's wholesale prices. Among these are: *Crystal Ale*, £1. 1s. for *18 gallons*; *XXXX Old*, *2s. per gallon or 72s. per Barrel*. Porter cost less.

68   We stand on the southern tip of the Green looking along Ulting Road. Photographed before 1921, when the Council houses were built, the card is dated August 1922. The pantiled roof on the right is Mr. Atkinson's bakehouse and the figure with the trade bike and basket may well have been delivering bread. Two more cottages adjoin (see No. 70), the last having a steeply-pitched roof and all since demolished. At Wickham View, the large house, Mrs. Hodges provided teas for cycling clubs and later rented a room to doctors from Witham and Maldon in which to hold their surgeries. Until Dr. Sidney Emerick arrived in 1952, there was no doctor resident in the village. A white fence fronts the Cross Keys beerhouse with its big shed at the rear and thatch once covered four of the cottages that follow. The house chimneys and outbuildings on the left mark Ivy Barns belonging to Mr. John Upson, a farming family long established in the village.

69   Mr William Steele, whose father, John, had been a butcher before him (see No. 10) stands outside his newly-built butcher's shop on the Green in 1930. He bought his cattle at Braintree market and butchered them himself on the premises, the open white gate beside him giving entry to the slaughter yard. Son William then took over, followed by grandsons, Percy and Derek Steele. The business closed in January 1976, to become first a chandler's shop and then a private house. In the background are the chimneys of Brewery House and next, beside the house with bay windows, is a small sweet shop. Both belonged to the White family. One of the two young men standing by the delivery van is Stan Wood, son of Mr. Henry Wood, market gardener and greengrocer (see No. 32). On the extreme left, next to the footpath leading to Church Road, a keen eye may detect the rear wheels and back of the baker's cart belonging to Lewis Atkinson.

70   We have reason to be grateful to the unknown photographer of this and the next card. Unwittingly he has provided us with a unique panoramic view of some of the old houses, west of the Green, which have since been demolished. With the assembled crowd (occasion unknown) we stand in Bovingtons Farm field near Maldon Road, where today the hawthorn hedge grows high. Beyond the hedge a large elm tree grows at the end of one of the three Council house gardens. Use of a lens will more clearly reveal a pair of semi-detached houses in the Ulting Road with the Cross Keys pub set back to their right while, half-hidden by the elm, is Wickham View. On the site of the row of cottages, one with a steeply-pitched roof, now stand two bungalows, Caltone and Attlast. Behind the vicar are Mr. Steele's butcher's shop, Chandlers, and Mr. White's house, Braemar. The last two are seen from a different angle in the preceding card.

71 The camera now pans out to capture the view of the Green beginning with Brewery House. Here, in the 1920s, visiting doctors from Witham and Maldon held surgeries, patients mounting the steps to enter through the white front door. The Brewery buildings are, here, still intact although no longer in use. On the sign that once proudly proclaimed Mr. Brown's Brewery business the faded paint reads: *Cycle & Motor Works*, while in the cottages next door lived two of the Bovington Farm horsemen, Mr. Wilks and Mr. Langstone. Now one dwelling, it is called Brewery Cottage and is followed by an existing, long, low bungalow and a pair of cottages. Directly opposite these and inside our field, is a walnut tree. Now fully grown, it is in the garden of Marneys, which was built, around 1954, for Mrs. Lucy Nettleton and her daughter, Joan. Tall elms stand etched against the sky and the tops of horse chestnut trees follow the line of Church Road.

72   The white fence seen outside the Cross Keys beerhouse in card No. 68 has disappeared and the pub stands open to the road. A sign has been erected in front of the small building to the left. Once, a cottage stood on the pub site, but at some time burned down and the beerhouse was built in its stead, the first known landlord being Alfred Lucking, a farmer. He died in 1879 appointing three trustees to pay the rents and profits to his wife, Martha, who survived until 1903. A bill of sale of that year informs us that there was a slaughter house among the outbuildings – perhaps the large shed seen in a previous card. By 1926, Hugh Poulton, whose father had been head brewer at Brown's Brewery (see No. 66) was landlord. The Cross Keys then had only one small bar and Mr. Poulton gave service through a small hatch directly from the barrels in the cellar. He held the tenancy for more than forty years.

73 The Council houses on the Green were built on land donated by John Wright Esq. of the Priory and the Reverend Townsend. An early tenant of No. 18 was Mr. Lindley Bott, who was a correspondent for several local newspapers. In the thatched cottage once lived Mr. Walter 'Dolly' Havis, the carrier, who fetched and carried goods, including fish and medicines, from Witham and Maldon. By placing a card bearing the letter 'H' in the front window villagers requiring his services ensured a call. He was lame, and he announced his arrival by blowing a whistle. Here, a horse and cart approaches the entrance to Mr. John Upson's farm, Ivy Barns, on the right. This family, which once lived at Bovington's Farm, has worked the land in the village for more than 140 years. Fences and hedges were then no mere garden ornamentation but necessary obstructions, at a time when sheep and cattle were driven on foot from the farm.

HATFIELD PEVEREL

74   Here, in 1929, we stand where the Ulting Road leads from the Green to Nounsley. The bungalow on the left was occupied by Mr. W. Steele, the middle one by his brother Alfred, writer of the book on the Church and Priory, while the furthest belonged to Mr. J. Strange and his wife Alice (Steele). This last stands next to today's children's recreation ground. Conflicting memories believe the horseman to be either Mr. Trenfield who worked for Mr. Upson of Ivy Barns Farm, or Mr. George Turnage, a cartage contractor. George undertook house removals, delivered coal from Moy's coal yard near the station, and carried parcels from the station itself. Before dustbins were in use he collected people's rubbish both locally and at Terling. For this he used an old tin bath, tipping it when full into the cart then dumping it into a pond hole next to his home in Berewood Terrace or in a nearby sandpit.

75   The Sportsman's Arms, called a beerhouse in the 1891 census, serves the hamlet of Hatfield Peverel known as Nounsley. On its Green, once much larger and where the chestnut tree still gives shade, a fair used to be held. Pictured around 1916 are some of the family of the landlord, Mr. William Rowe, seated outside in the sunshine with their small dog, Fluff. Mr. Bill Doe wheels his bicycle from the footpath leading to the Garden Fields and the Ford. Each year in the early 1920s some friends of Mr. Hester of Red Robins, boot and shoe repairer, arrived at the pub on fishing expeditions. A fleet of thirty London taxis brought them and their tackle. In the First World War troops filled Priory Park, at the rear of the beerhouse, while an artillery troop was billeted at Priory Farm, then owned by Mr. Upson. A German spy who had been poisoning water in the horse troughs was discovered by Mrs. Rowe. He was hiding in her cellar!

Nounsley
Hatfield Peverel

76   For more than a hundred years the windmill dominated the skyline on the high ridge between the Rivers Ter and Chelmer. Its site can be identified by the miller's cottage (now with only one chimney) which still stands at the entrance of the driveway to Gardener's Farm at Nounsley. In this rare photograph of 1928 the size of the mill is given scale by the horse and hayrake in the adjoining meadow. Seated at the reins is Jack Clemence, whose brother Charles still lives in the village. Gardener's Farm was held by the Bott family until the late 1800s and the mill, which appears in a sale notice dated July 1886, was in use until 1897. The sails, although no longer needed, continued to rotate noisily in the strong winds that blew along the ridge causing some alarm so, around 1900, the canvas shutters were removed. In 1942, the mill, an obvious landmark for German bombers heading for Chelmsford and London, was totally demolished. A sad loss.